How to Buy Amazon Return Pallets for Beginners 2024

A Comprehensive Guide to Buying, Reselling, and Profiting from Amazon Liquidation pallets, simple ways to making money from return pallets on amazon.

Susan Harrison

CONTENTS

INTRODUCTION

Have you ever wondered what happens to products that are returned to Amazon?

Well, you're about to discover an untapped resource that can turn these seemingly unwanted goods into a lucrative venture.

In today's world of online shopping, the volume of returns is staggering. Customers send back products for various reasons, such as receiving the wrong item, not being satisfied with the product's quality, or simply changing their minds. These returned items are then collected, categorized, and made available through Amazon's liquidation program.

The concept of buying and reselling Amazon return pallets is not only a smart business move but also an environmentally conscious one. By participating in the liquidation market, you are contributing to the reduction of waste and the promotion of a circular economy. Instead of these items ending up in landfills, you have the opportunity to breathe new life into them and provide value to customers who are seeking affordable options.

Throughout the pages of this book, "How to buy Amazon return pallets for beginners 2024" we will guide you through the entire process, from understanding the intricacies of Amazon return pallets to sourcing, inspecting, and reselling the products. We will explore different sales channels, pricing strategies, and marketing techniques to help you maximize your returns. Additionally, we'll provide insights into refurbishing and repairing items, ensuring that your products are in optimal condition for resale.

Let's dive in and discover the simple ways to earn money using Amazon liquidation pallets!

CHAPTER 1

UNDERSTANDING AMAZON RETURN PALLETS

What are Amazon return pallets?

Amazon return pallets are large palletized loads of merchandise that have been returned to Amazon by customers for various reasons. These pallets contain a mix of items from different categories, including electronics, home goods, clothing, toys, and more. When customers return items to Amazon, whether due to damage, defects, buyer's remorse, or other reasons, the returned items are often sorted, evaluated, and repackaged into pallet-sized loads for resale.

Types of products found in return pallets

Amazon return pallets can contain a wide variety of products, including but not limited to:

Electronics: Such as smartphones, tablets, laptops, cameras, and accessories.

- Home goods: Including small appliances, kitchenware, bedding, and decor items.

- Clothing and accessories: Ranging from apparel for men, women, and children to footwear and accessories.
- Toys and games: Including board games, action figures, puzzles, and outdoor play equipment.
- Health and beauty products: Such as skincare, haircare, cosmetics, and grooming essentials.
- Sports and outdoor equipment: Including fitness gear, camping supplies, and recreational equipment.
- Books and media: Such as books, DVDs, CDs, and video games.
- Seasonal items: Such as holiday decorations, costumes, and party supplies.
- Miscellaneous items: Such as office supplies, pet products, and automotive accessories.

Condition of products in return pallets

The condition of items in Amazon return pallets can vary widely due to the nature of customer returns. Some items may be brand new and still in their original packaging, while others may have minor damage or signs of wear. Common conditions of products found in return pallets include:

- Like new: Items that appear unused and are in excellent condition with no visible signs of wear.
- Open box: Items that have been opened but are still in good condition with all original accessories and packaging.
- Used: Items that show signs of wear or use but are still functional and usable.
- Damaged: Items with visible damage or defects that may require repair or refurbishment.
- Unsalvageable: Items that are too damaged or defective to be resold and may need to be disposed of or recycled.

Reasons for products being returned to Amazon

Products end up being returned to Amazon for a variety of reasons, including but not limited to:

- Product defects or malfunctions: Customers may return items that are faulty, damaged, or not working as expected.
- Damage during shipping or handling: Items may be returned due to damage sustained during shipping or mishandling by carriers.

- Customer dissatisfaction: Customers may return items if they are not satisfied with the quality, fit, color, or functionality of the product.
- Buyer's remorse: Customers may return items due to changing their minds or realizing they no longer need or want the product.
- Seasonal or clearance items: Products may be returned after seasonal events or clearance sales, especially if they were purchased impulsively or on sale.
- Overstock or excess inventory: Amazon may receive returns of items that were overstocked or ordered in excess and are no longer needed in their inventory.

CHAPTER 2

FINDING AND SOURCING AMAZON RETURN PALLETS

Amazon's liquidation program

Amazon offers its own liquidation program where buyers can purchase return pallets directly from the company. Through this program, buyers can access a wide range of merchandise returned to Amazon's fulfillment centers. These auctions typically occur after holiday sales when return volumes are high. Amazon's liquidation program offers transparency regarding the condition of items and provides detailed manifests outlining the contents of each pallet. Buyers can purchase pallets individually or in bulk, and shipping options may vary depending on location.

Online liquidation marketplaces

There are several online liquidation marketplaces that specialize in selling returned merchandise, including Amazon return pallets. These platforms connect buyers with sellers who source and liquidate inventory from various sources, including Amazon, retailers, and manufacturers.

Popular online liquidation marketplaces include:

- Liquidation.com
- BULQ
- Wholesale Ninjas
- Direct Liquidation
- Quicklotz
- Amazon Liquidation Auctions
- BlueLots
- 888Lots
- Via Trading

Liquidation.com

Liquidation.com (US) operates similarly to Direct Liquidation, offering a platform for the sale of return pallets sourced from Amazon and various other marketplaces. The inventory on this platform typically consists of electronics, household appliances, computers, and industrial and vehicle spare parts.

Prices for pallets usually start at $100 but can vary and increase during auctions.

For non-US customers, payment is typically accepted via wire transfer. Additionally, for purchases exceeding $5,000, wire transfer is mandatory for both US and non-US buyers.

Pros:

- Liquidation.com provides access to great deals on return pallets, potentially allowing buyers to acquire items at a lower cost than their original retail price.
- Buyers may discover valuable and resalable items within the pallets, providing opportunities for profit.

Cons:

- Warranty coverage or guarantees for the condition or functionality of purchased items may vary depending on the product or seller.
- Due to the platform's popularity, buyers may encounter stiff competition during auctions, leading to elevated prices or difficulty in securing desired items.

BULQ

BULQ, headquartered in the United States, is a prominent liquidation company known for listing new return pallets for sale three times daily. The pricing of these items varies based on the seller and product category, with some prices being fixed, while others are sold through a 48-hour auction.

While browsing the clearance section on BULQ is accessible without logging in, purchasing requires registration on the platform and providing resale certification during the transaction process.

BULQ also offers shipping services for addresses within the United States, often applying a flat shipping fee of $30. However, shipping costs may vary based on factors such as weight, pallet size, and delivery address.

Pros:

- BULQ offers a diverse range of products sourced from big-box store retailers across categories like apparel, home and garden, toys and baby, electronics, and more.

- With new inventory arriving three times daily, sellers have continuous opportunities to explore and purchase items.
- The platform is tailored for resellers, offering bulk purchasing options, discounted pricing, and access to a community of fellow resellers.

Cons:

- As with any liquidation platform, there is a risk of purchasing damaged or defective products unsuitable for resale.
- While manifest information is provided, buyers may have limited ability to customize or select specific items within a pallet.
- Buyers are responsible for arranging shipping and handling costs, which can vary depending on location and pallet size.

Direct liquidation

Direct Liquidation is a dynamic liquidation marketplace that collaborates with major retailers such as Amazon, Target, and Walmart to facilitate online auctions for returned pallets.

One standout feature of this platform is its ability to refine searches by store and brand. For instance, buyers can easily filter for return pallets exclusively from Amazon, streamlining the sourcing process.

Direct Liquidation operates solely through auctions, requiring users to register and place bids to secure desired pallets.

Pros:

- Direct Liquidation boasts a diverse array of liquidation pallets spanning categories like electronics, appliances, furniture, and more.
- Partnering directly with prominent retailers and marketplaces ensures the authenticity of the products available on the platform.
- The platform prides itself on delivering exceptional customer service to buyers, fostering a positive purchasing experience.

Cons:

- As with any liquidation purchase, there is no guarantee regarding the condition of the products received.
- Some pallets within specific categories may have minimum quantity restrictions, limiting accessibility for small-scale buyers.
- Depending on the condition of the item, warranty coverage for purchased products may be limited or nonexistent.

Amazon liquidation Auction

In 2018, Amazon teamed up with B-Stock to introduce Amazon Liquidation Auctions, providing third-party US sellers with the opportunity to bid on return pallets encompassing a wide range of categories, including books, apparel, home goods, electronics, and footwear.

To participate in these auctions, sellers are required to register with B-Stock and submit a valid resale certificate.

Here are some pros and cons of Amazon Liquidation Auction:

Pros:

- Purchasing customer returns through Amazon Liquidation can often be more cost-effective than sourcing new merchandise, enabling businesses to maximize profit margins.
- Merchandise acquired from Amazon Liquidation auctions is frequently in as-new condition, enhancing the profit potential for resellers.
- Amazon Liquidation auctions offer the option to buy in bulk, which can help mitigate costs for businesses.

Cons:

- Auctions can be time-consuming to execute, typically requiring at least two to three business days, which may pose challenges for larger companies with limited bandwidth to monitor them closely.
- Not all buyers prefer to engage in auctions due to the time commitment and unpredictability of the outcome, leading to potential hesitation among some sellers.
- Despite the potential for profitability, there is always a risk of receiving damaged or unsellable items when purchasing liquidation

stock, which could result in financial losses for buyers.

888Lots

888Lots stands as one of the oldest liquidation companies in the USA, offering buyers the flexibility to purchase products in bulk or as individual items at discounted rates.

One notable feature of 888Lots is the ability for buyers to customize lots and select specific items according to their needs.

To make purchases on the platform, buyers must provide a valid resale certificate, enabling them to sell to US customers legally.

Pros:

- 888Lots boasts an extensive inventory of over 100,000 brand-new products spanning across more than 30 categories.
- The platform offers fixed-priced pallets, with buyers having the option to negotiate prices with their assigned sales representative.
- Each pallet includes a detailed description of the products, including ASIN numbers, UPCs,

descriptions, reviews, sales rank, and a downloadable manifest.

Cons:

- There is no guarantee regarding the condition of products received after purchase, posing a potential risk for buyers.
- Buyers are responsible for covering shipping and handling costs after purchasing pallets, which can impact overall expenses.

In addition to these leading liquidation platforms, several others also specialize in selling Amazon Return Pallets, including Via Trading (US), Quicklotz (US), Wholesale Ninjas (US), and BlueLots. These platforms offer buyers further options for sourcing liquidation inventory to meet their business needs.

It's essential to review each platform's policies, fees, and shipping options before making a purchase.

Local liquidation auctions and sales

Buyers can also find Amazon return pallets through local liquidation auctions and sales. These events may be organized by liquidation companies, wholesalers, or retailers looking to offload excess inventory. Local auctions and sales provide an opportunity for buyers to inspect pallets in person before making a purchase, which can be beneficial for assessing the condition and quality of items. Additionally, buyers may be able to negotiate prices and arrange for local pickup, reducing shipping costs.

Evaluating the credibility of liquidation sources

When sourcing Amazon return pallets, it's crucial to evaluate the credibility and reputation of liquidation sources. Factors to consider include:

- **Transparency:** Look for sellers or platforms that provide detailed manifests, photos, and descriptions of pallet contents.
- **Customer reviews**: Check for reviews and testimonials from other buyers to gauge their experiences with the seller or platform.

- **Return policies:** Review the seller's return policies, including any conditions or restrictions on returning merchandise.
- **Payment security:** Ensure that payment transactions are secure and that the seller or platform offers reliable payment methods.
- **Communication:** Evaluate the seller's responsiveness and communication regarding inquiries, orders, and shipping updates.

Factors to consider when sourcing pallets

When purchasing Amazon Return Pallets, it's essential to keep several factors in mind to ensure a profitable experience and minimize potential risks. Here are some key considerations:

1. Compare liquidation platforms:

Research and compare different liquidation companies to find the ones offering return pallets at competitive prices. This helps maximize profit margins and ensures you're getting the best value for your investment.

2. Start with a small purchase:

Before committing to large investments, start with a small initial purchase. This allows you to familiarize yourself with the buying process and gauge the overall experience. Avoid immediately investing in expensive name-brand goods, as it can pose higher risks for newcomers.

3. Be cautious with electronics:

If you're new to buying Amazon liquidation pallets, exercise caution when purchasing pallets containing used electronic items. These items may have a higher likelihood of being non-functional, and if you lack the expertise to repair them, it could result in a total loss.

4. Avoid certain categories:

Minimize risks by avoiding certain categories of products, such as baby items (due to safety concerns) and cooking products (which may be difficult to resell). Additionally, steer clear of products with multiple parts or accessories, as there's a higher chance of missing or damaged components.

5. Look for simplicity:

Opt for simpler items with a higher likelihood of working properly and being easy to resell. For example, exercise dumbbells can be a good option. While name-brand goods are desirable, ensure the probability of defects is low, particularly when it comes to electronics.

6. Watch out for shipping costs:

Before finalizing a purchase, carefully consider the shipping expenses associated with the Amazon return pallet or any other type of liquidation pallet. Some liquidation companies may charge significant shipping fees, which could potentially exceed the amount paid for the goods. Always review the freight costs in advance to avoid unexpected surprises and ensure cost-effectiveness.

CHAPTER 3

ASSESSING THE PROFITABILITY OF AMAZON RETURN PALLETS

Determining the potential resale value of pallets

Assessing the potential resale value of Amazon return pallets involves evaluating the condition, contents, and market demand for the items within the pallet. Factors to consider include:

- Condition: Determine the overall condition of the items, ranging from brand new to used or damaged.
- Contents: Review the manifest to identify the types of products included in the pallet and their respective brands, categories, and quantities.
- Market demand: Research the demand for similar products in the resale market and consider factors such as seasonality, trends, and consumer preferences.

Calculating profit margins and return on investment

Calculating profit margins and return on investment (ROI) is essential for determining the profitability of Amazon return pallets. Key steps include:

- Cost analysis: Calculate the total cost of acquiring the pallet, including purchase price, shipping fees, and any additional expenses.
- Revenue estimation: Estimate the potential revenue from reselling the items within the pallet, taking into account pricing strategies, market demand, and sales channels.
- Profit margin calculation: Determine the difference between total revenue and total costs to calculate the profit margin percentage.
- ROI calculation: Divide the net profit by the total investment (purchase cost) and multiply by 100 to calculate the ROI percentage. This indicates the return earned relative to the initial investment.

Analyzing demand and market trends

Analyzing demand and market trends is crucial for identifying profitable opportunities and optimizing resale strategies. Key considerations include:

- Product demand: Research the demand for specific product categories or items within the Amazon return pallets, considering factors such as consumer preferences, seasonal trends, and emerging markets.
- Market trends: Stay informed about market trends, including pricing fluctuations, competitor analysis, and emerging consumer behaviors, to capitalize on profitable opportunities and adapt strategies accordingly.
- Sales channels: Explore various sales channels, including online marketplaces, brick-and-mortar stores, flea markets, and wholesale distribution, to reach target customers and maximize sales potential.

CHAPTER 4

INSPECTING AND SORTING AMAZON RETURN PALLETS

Essential tools for inspecting pallets

When inspecting Amazon return pallets, having the right tools can streamline the process and ensure thorough evaluation. Essential tools include:

- Flashlight: To inspect items in dimly lit areas or inside packaging.
- Box cutter or utility knife: For opening boxes and packages to examine contents.
- Tape measure: To check dimensions of larger items and ensure they meet buyer expectations.
- Gloves: To protect hands while handling potentially damaged or dirty items.
- Testing equipment: Depending on the product categories, testing equipment such as multimeters for electronics or pressure gauges for appliances may be necessary.
- Manifest: A detailed list of items included in the pallet to cross-reference during inspection.

Evaluating the condition of products

Inspecting the condition of products within Amazon return pallets is critical for determining their resale value. Key steps for evaluating product condition include:

- Visual inspection: Examine items for visible damage, wear and tear, or signs of use.
- Functionality testing: Test electronic devices, appliances, and other functional items to ensure they are in working order.
- Cosmetic assessment: Check for scratches, dents, or cosmetic imperfections that may affect resale value.
- Completeness verification: Confirm that all parts, accessories, and components are present and accounted for, especially for items sold as complete sets or bundles.

Sorting products for resale, refurbishment, or disposal

After inspection, sorting products into appropriate categories helps streamline the resale process and optimize profitability. Sorting options include:

- **Resale:** Items in good condition and fully functional can be listed for resale through various channels, maximizing revenue potential.
- **Refurbishment:** Products that require minor repairs or refurbishment can be restored to like-new condition and sold at a higher price point.
- **Salvage:** Items that are damaged beyond repair or missing essential components may be designated for disposal or salvage, minimizing losses and freeing up space for profitable inventory.

CHAPTER 5

RESELLING AMAZON RETURN PRODUCTS

Choosing the right sales channels

Selecting the appropriate sales channels is crucial for effectively reselling Amazon return products. Consider the following options:

- Online marketplaces: Platforms like eBay, Amazon Marketplace, and Shopify offer broad reach and access to a large customer base.
- Wholesale distribution: Partnering with wholesalers or retailers can provide access to brick-and-mortar stores and expand market reach.
- Flea markets and trade shows: Local events offer opportunities to connect with buyers directly and showcase products in person.
- Social media platforms: Utilize social media platforms like Facebook Marketplace, Instagram, and Twitter to promote products and engage with potential customers.

Setting competitive pricing strategies

Implementing competitive pricing strategies is essential for attracting customers and maximizing sales. Consider the following pricing tactics:

- Research competitors: Analyze pricing trends on similar products within your niche to determine competitive price points.
- Pricing tiers: Offer multiple pricing tiers to cater to different customer segments, including budget-friendly options and premium packages.
- Promotions and discounts: Implement promotional offers, such as discounts, bundle deals, or free shipping, to incentivize purchases and drive sales.
- Dynamic pricing: Utilize dynamic pricing strategies to adjust prices in real-time based on demand, market trends, and competitor pricing.

Marketing and advertising your products

Effective marketing and advertising strategies are essential for increasing product visibility and driving sales. Consider the following tactics:

- Search engine optimization (SEO): Optimize product listings with relevant keywords, high-quality images, and detailed descriptions to improve search engine rankings.

- Social media marketing: Leverage social media platforms to showcase products, engage with customers, and run targeted advertising campaigns.
- Email marketing: Build and nurture an email subscriber list to send promotional offers, product updates, and exclusive discounts to interested customers.
- Influencer partnerships: Collaborate with influencers and bloggers in your niche to promote products and reach a wider audience.

Managing customer returns and refunds

Efficiently managing customer returns and refunds is crucial for maintaining customer satisfaction and reputation. Consider the following best practices:

- Clear return policy: Establish a transparent and customer-friendly return policy outlining terms and conditions, including return window, refund options, and eligibility criteria.
- Streamlined return process: Implement an easy-to-use return process with clear instructions and

dedicated customer support to assist with returns and exchanges.

- Timely refunds: Process refunds promptly upon receipt of returned items to ensure a positive customer experience and encourage repeat business.
- Product inspection: Thoroughly inspect returned items to assess their condition and determine whether they can be resold, refurbished, or salvaged.

CHAPTER 6

REFURBISHING AND REPAIRING AMAZON RETURN PRODUCTS

Common refurbishment techniques

Refurbishing Amazon return products can significantly enhance their value and resale potential. Common refurbishment techniques include:

- Cleaning and sanitizing: Thoroughly clean and sanitize products to remove dirt, dust, and stains, improving their appearance and hygiene.
- Testing and troubleshooting: Test electronic devices, appliances, and other functional items to identify and address any performance issues or malfunctions.
- Replacement of parts: Replace damaged or missing parts, components, or accessories to restore products to optimal functionality.
- Cosmetic repairs: Repair cosmetic imperfections such as scratches, dents, or scuffs to improve product aesthetics and appeal.

Repairing damaged products

Repairing damaged Amazon return products requires skill, expertise, and attention to detail. Key steps in repairing damaged products include:

- Assessing damage: Thoroughly inspect products to identify the extent of damage and determine the necessary repairs.
- Repairing structural damage: Address structural damage such as cracks, breaks, or fractures using appropriate repair techniques and materials.
- Fixing mechanical issues: Diagnose and repair mechanical issues such as jammed mechanisms, faulty switches, or malfunctioning components.
- Soldering and wiring: Perform soldering and wiring repairs for electronic devices and appliances to fix connectivity issues or damaged circuits.

Enhancing product aesthetics and functionality

Enhancing the aesthetics and functionality of Amazon return products can increase their desirability and market value. Techniques for enhancing product aesthetics and functionality include:

- Refinishing surfaces: Refinish surfaces using painting, staining, or polishing techniques to improve appearance and restore original luster.
- Upgrading features: Upgrade product features or functionalities to add value and appeal, such as installing new hardware or adding smart technology.
- Customization options: Offer customization options such as personalized engravings, custom colors, or accessory upgrades to cater to customer preferences.
- Quality assurance testing: Conduct thorough quality assurance testing to ensure refurbished products meet or exceed industry standards and customer expectations.

CHAPTER 7

DEALING WITH UNSOLD OR UNSALVAGEABLE PRODUCTS

Liquidation options for unsold products

When faced with unsold or unsalvageable products, exploring liquidation options can help recoup some of the investment and clear inventory. Consider the following liquidation options:

- Liquidation auctions: Participate in liquidation auctions to sell unsold products in bulk to other buyers or liquidation companies.
- Wholesale clearance sales: Offer unsold products at discounted prices to wholesale buyers or retailers looking to purchase large quantities.
- Online marketplace listings: List unsold products on online marketplaces such as eBay, Craigslist, or Facebook Marketplace to reach individual buyers.

Recycling and disposal considerations

For products that cannot be sold or salvaged, proper recycling and disposal are essential to minimize environmental impact. Consider the following recycling and disposal options:

- Recycling programs: Partner with recycling companies or organizations that specialize in recycling electronic waste, plastics, metals, and other recyclable materials.
- Donation programs: Donate unsold products to charitable organizations, schools, or community centers that may have use for them or can repurpose them for other purposes.
- Responsible disposal: Dispose of unsalvageable products responsibly by following local regulations and guidelines for hazardous waste disposal or landfill disposal.

Minimizing waste and environmental impact

To minimize waste and environmental impact, consider implementing the following strategies:

- Sustainable packaging: Use eco-friendly packaging materials such as recycled cardboard, biodegradable plastics, or reusable packaging options.

- Product lifecycle assessment: Conduct a thorough assessment of the product lifecycle to identify areas where waste can be minimized, such as reducing packaging materials or implementing product design changes.
- Circular economy initiatives: Explore opportunities to participate in circular economy initiatives, such as product refurbishment programs, take-back schemes, or product recycling programs, to extend the lifespan of products and reduce waste.

CHAPTER 8

TIPS FOR SUCCESSFUL OPERATIONS

Developing a business plan and strategy

Developing a comprehensive business plan and strategy is essential for guiding your operations and achieving long-term success. Consider the following tips:

- Define your business goals and objectives: Clearly outline your short-term and long-term goals, including financial targets, growth milestones, and market expansion plans.
- Conduct market research: Analyze market trends, customer preferences, and competitor strategies to identify opportunities and challenges in your industry.
- Outline your business model: Define your target market, product offerings, pricing strategies, and distribution channels to create a roadmap for your business operations.
- Establish key performance indicators (KPIs): Set measurable KPIs to track your progress and

evaluate the success of your business strategy over time.

Managing inventory and logistics

Effective inventory and logistics management are crucial for optimizing operational efficiency and meeting customer demands. Consider the following tips:

- Implement inventory tracking systems: Utilize inventory management software or systems to track stock levels, monitor product movements, and streamline order fulfillment processes.
- Optimize warehouse operations: Organize your warehouse layout for maximum efficiency, implement inventory labeling and shelving systems, and establish clear inventory control procedures.
- Invest in reliable logistics partners: Partner with reputable logistics providers to ensure timely delivery, minimize shipping costs, and enhance customer satisfaction.

Tips for Selling Amazon Return Pallets

Now that you're eager to dive into selling Amazon Return Pallets, it's essential to keep a few key tips in mind to ensure success in 2024. Here are some valuable pointers:

Compare products across different marketplaces:

Before committing to a liquidation pallet, take the time to compare offerings from various liquidation companies. Look for pallets offered at competitive prices. If possible, attend offline auctions to inspect pallets firsthand, enabling you to assess each one and negotiate favorable pricing.

Factor shipping costs into your calculations to avoid potential profit depletion.

Sort and categorize items effectively:

Upon receiving your pallet, conduct a thorough inspection and categorize the products accordingly. Evaluate the packaging and condition of each item, verifying authenticity and the presence of manufacturer warranties.

Address any missing or faulty parts promptly through replacement or repair to enhance product sellability and increase resale value.

Bundle complementary products:

In addition to refurbishing and repairing individual items, consider bundling complementary products to boost the average order value. For instance, assembling a CPU with a mix of new and refurbished components from a pallet of computer parts can command a premium price.

Price your products strategically:

Research prices across various online markets to gauge the current market value of your products. Set your selling price below that of new items, factoring in additional expenses such as shipping and handling. Keep a close eye on potential profits to ensure profitability.

Choose between manifested and mystery pallets:

When selecting pallets, weigh the options between manifested and mystery pallets. While mystery pallets are cheaper, they entail higher risk due to uncertainty about the contents. Conversely, manifested pallets, though pricier, provide detailed descriptions of contents, including item names, quantities, descriptions, and retail values. For resale purposes, manifested pallets offer greater transparency and are the preferred choice.

CHAPTER 9

POTENTIAL CHALLENGES AND RISKS

Common challenges in the liquidation business

Navigating the liquidation business comes with its share of challenges. Here are some common ones you might encounter:

- Inconsistent product quality: Products in liquidation pallets can vary widely in quality, leading to uncertainty about the condition of items and potential resale value.
- High competition: The liquidation market is competitive, with many sellers vying for the same inventory. This can lead to bidding wars and inflated prices, impacting profitability.
- Limited warranty and returns: Unlike new products, items in liquidation pallets may not come with warranties or return policies, making it challenging to address customer concerns and returns.
- Shipping and logistics issues: Managing shipping logistics for large quantities of

inventory can be complex and costly, especially when dealing with oversized or heavy items.

Mitigating risks and minimizing losses

To mitigate risks and minimize losses in the liquidation business, consider implementing the following strategies:

- Thorough inspection and testing: Conduct comprehensive inspections and testing of products to identify defects or issues before resale. This helps minimize the risk of selling faulty or non-functional items to customers.
- Diversification of inventory sources: Avoid relying too heavily on a single liquidation source. Diversifying your inventory sources can help reduce dependence on any one supplier and mitigate the impact of fluctuations in product quality or availability.
- Strategic pricing and margin management: Set pricing strategies that account for potential losses due to damaged or unsellable items. Maintain a healthy profit margin to absorb unexpected costs and mitigate the impact of low-margin sales.

- Customer service and satisfaction: Prioritize excellent customer service and satisfaction to build trust and loyalty with buyers. Promptly address any issues or concerns raised by customers to minimize negative feedback and mitigate reputational risks.

Legal and compliance considerations

Operating in the liquidation business requires adherence to legal and compliance standards. Consider the following considerations:

- Product authenticity and legality: Ensure that products sold through liquidation channels are authentic and legally obtained. Avoid dealing with counterfeit or stolen goods to prevent legal repercussions.
- Consumer protection laws: Familiarize yourself with consumer protection laws and regulations governing the sale of goods, warranties, and returns. Comply with legal requirements to avoid potential fines or penalties.
- Environmental regulations: Dispose of unsalvageable or damaged inventory responsibly, following environmental

regulations and guidelines for hazardous waste disposal and recycling.

CHAPTER 10

CASE STUDIES AND SUCCESS STORIES

Real-life examples of successful ventures

Examining real-life examples of successful ventures in the liquidation business can provide valuable insights and inspiration. Here are a few examples:

Case Study 1: John's Electronics Resale

John, an experienced liquidator, specializes in reselling electronics obtained through liquidation pallets. By thoroughly inspecting and refurbishing items, John has built a thriving online business selling smartphones, tablets, and laptops. Through strategic pricing and excellent customer service, John has cultivated a loyal customer base and achieved consistent sales growth.

Case Study 2: Sarah's Wholesale Clothing

Sarah, a newcomer to the liquidation industry, launched her wholesale clothing business by sourcing inventory from liquidation pallets. By curating trendy and high-quality clothing items, Sarah has attracted boutique owners and online retailers seeking affordable inventory. Through savvy marketing and networking, Sarah has expanded her customer base and established herself as a trusted supplier in the fashion industry.

Case Study 3: Mark's Home Goods Outlet

Mark operates a successful home goods outlet, specializing in furniture and decor sourced from liquidation auctions. With a keen eye for quality and design, Mark refurbishes and displays items in his showroom, attracting homeowners and interior designers seeking unique pieces at discounted prices. Through effective merchandising and word-of-mouth referrals, Mark has achieved steady sales and positive reviews.

Lessons learned from experienced liquidators

Drawing lessons from experienced liquidators can provide valuable insights into best practices and strategies for success. Here are some key lessons learned:

Lesson 1: Thorough inspection is key: Experienced liquidators emphasize the importance of conducting thorough inspections and testing of products to ensure quality and functionality before resale.

Lesson 2: Build relationships with suppliers: Establishing strong relationships with reputable suppliers and wholesalers is essential for accessing high-quality inventory and securing favorable pricing terms.

Lesson 3: Prioritize customer satisfaction: Providing excellent customer service and addressing customer concerns promptly are critical for building trust and loyalty with buyers and fostering long-term relationships.

Lesson 4: Adapt to market trends: Successful liquidators stay abreast of market trends and consumer preferences, adjusting their inventory and pricing strategies accordingly to meet changing demand.

CONCLUSION

As you embark on your journey into the world of Amazon return pallets and liquidation business, remember that success doesn't happen overnight. It requires dedication, perseverance, and a willingness to learn from both successes and failures.

Stay informed, stay adaptable, and stay committed to providing value to your customers. By following the strategies and insights outlined in this guide, you'll be well-equipped to navigate the challenges and capitalize on the opportunities in the liquidation industry.

Selling Amazon Return Pallets can be a lucrative endeavor, but it's crucial to acknowledge the associated risks.

While some pallets may yield profitable items, others might contain damaged or defective goods.

Successful resale of Amazon Return Pallets requires meticulous inspection, sorting, pricing, and effective marketing strategies.

For sellers who thrive on challenges, delving into the world of liquidation items can offer an exciting opportunity.

Now equipped with the knowledge of selling Amazon Return Pallets, it's time to dive in and embark on this entrepreneurial journey. With determination and the right approach, you can transform these pallets into profitable ventures for your business. Best of luck as you venture into this dynamic marketplace!

Above all, believe in yourself and your ability to succeed. With determination and effort, you have the potential to build a thriving business and achieve your goals.

Good luck on your entrepreneurial journey!

Made in the USA
Monee, IL
19 September 2024